10/00

FRIENDS
OF ACPL

D1162141

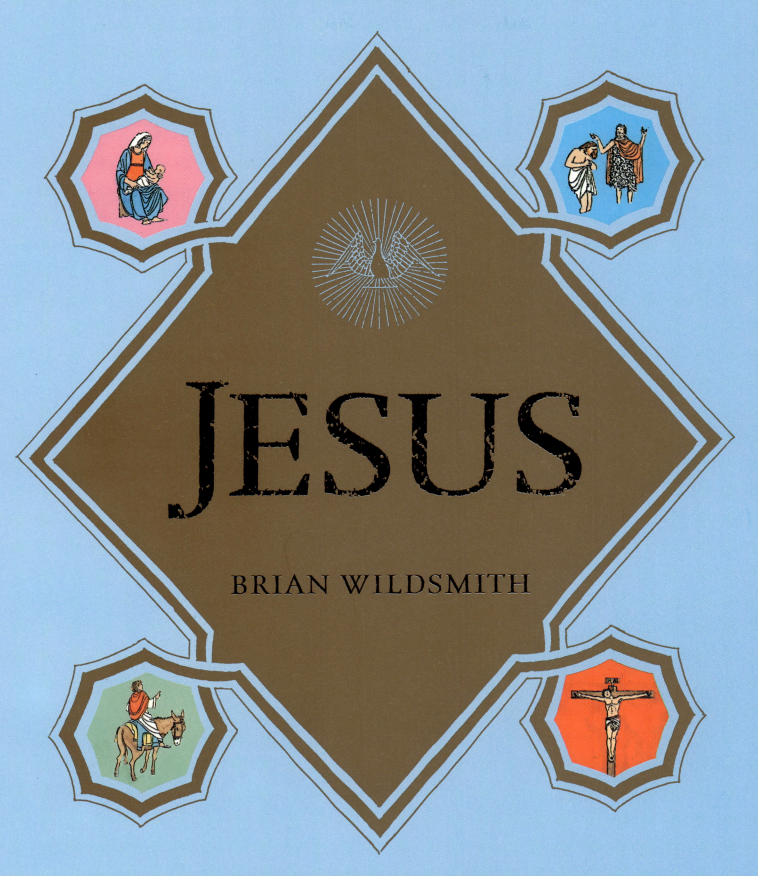

JESUS

BRIAN WILDSMITH

Eerdmans Books for Young Readers

Grand Rapids, Michigan / Cambridge, U.K.

The angel Gabriel was sent by God to Mary, a young girl who lived in Nazareth. "God has chosen you," said the angel. "You will have a son, and you will name him Jesus. He will be the Son of God."

Some time later, Mary had to make a long journey to Bethlehem with her husband, Joseph.

They had to sleep in a stable because there was no room for them in the inn.
    And there, surrounded by animals, Mary's son was born under the light of a shining star.

Shepherds were guarding their sheep when angels appeared in the sky. The angels told them the good news that the Son of God had been born in Bethlehem.

The shepherds hurried to Bethlehem and found Mary and Joseph and the baby, who was lying in a manger.

Meanwhile, three wise men from the East came to see King Herod. "Where is the newborn King of the Jews?" they asked. "We have seen his star."

The chief priests replied, "The prophets say he will be born in Bethlehem."

Then Herod told the wise men, "Go and find the child. Then come back and tell me."

The wise men traveled on, following the star until it stopped above the place where the little child was. They went in and opened their treasure chests.

They gave Jesus gifts of gold, frankincense, and myrrh.

That night an angel appeared to Joseph and said, "Take Mary and the baby to Egypt. Herod's soldiers are looking for Jesus. They want to kill him." So Joseph got up and took Mary and Jesus to Egypt.

The wise men had been warned in a dream not to go back to Herod, so they returned to their own country by a different road.

After Herod's death, Jesus' family returned to Nazareth. When Jesus was twelve, his parents took him to Jerusalem for the Feast of Passover. When it was over, Mary and Joseph set off for home but didn't realize that Jesus wasn't with them. They went back and found Jesus in the temple, asking the teachers questions. Everyone was amazed.

The years passed. A prophet, John, invited people to be baptized in the Jordan River to show that they wanted to lead a new life.

Jesus left his home in Nazareth and was baptized by John in the river. The Spirit of God appeared like a dove, and a voice from heaven said, "You are my dear son."

Satan came to tempt Jesus in the desert. "If you're hungry," said Satan, "turn these stones into bread." But Jesus refused. Satan then took him to the roof of the temple. "Throw yourself down," said Satan. "God's angels will protect you." Again Jesus refused. Satan then showed Jesus all the kingdoms of the world. "All this shall be yours if you worship me," he said.

"You should not tempt God," said Jesus. And Satan left him.

Jesus returned home and went with his mother to a wedding in Cana. The wine ran out before the party was over. "Fill these jars with water," said Jesus. When the guests tasted it, the water had turned into very fine wine.

Later, Jesus was walking by the Sea of Galilee and saw Simon Peter and his brother, Andrew, fishing. "Follow me," said Jesus. "From now on, you will be fishers of men."

One day Jesus was out on Peter's fishing boat. "Throw your net into the water," said Jesus.

"We've caught nothing all night," said Peter. But Peter threw the net into the water, and it came up full of fish.

Near a town called Nain, men were carrying out a young man who had just died. He was his mother's only son, and she was a widow. Jesus said, "Young man, rise up." The man sat up and began to speak.

Jesus then chose twelve special friends to be with him and to help him with his work. He called them his disciples.

He sat down on the top of a hill and taught them, together with the crowds of people who came to hear the good news about God.

One night, Jesus was with his friends on a boat. He was very tired and fell asleep. When a fierce storm came his friends woke him. Jesus called to the wind and rain, "Be still." And suddenly it was calm.

On the other side of the lake Jesus taught the crowds. By evening everyone was hungry. "We only have five loaves and two fish," said the disciples. "And there are five thousand people here."

"Tell them all to sit down," said Jesus. Then he blessed the loaves and fish. The disciples passed the food around, and everyone had enough to eat. The food that was left over filled twelve baskets.

Jesus was called to the home of a man named Jairus. He was sad because his daughter had died. "Little girl," said Jesus gently, "it's time to get up." She opened her eyes and got up.

The disciples were out on a boat one night and saw Jesus walking towards them on the water. Peter leaped overboard and tried to walk on the water too, but he started to sink. "Have faith, Peter," Jesus said and saved him.

Later Jesus asked Peter, "Who do you think I am?"

"You are the Christ," said Peter, "the Son of God."

"God has revealed this to you," said Jesus. "You will be the leader of the church."

One day Jesus took Peter, James, and John to the top of a high mountain. There the disciples saw Jesus change. His clothes became dazzling white, and the disciples saw Moses and Elijah talking with Jesus.

A voice from heaven said, "This is my dear son. Listen to him." And then the disciples were alone again on the mountain with Jesus.

Jesus received a message from two sisters, Mary and Martha, saying that their brother, Lazarus, was very ill. When Jesus arrived, the sisters told him Lazarus had died.

Jesus told the people to take the stone away from the tomb. Then he called, "Lazarus, come out." And Lazarus came out, wrapped in white linen.

Another day parents brought children to Jesus. His disciples told them to go away, but Jesus said, "Let the children come to me. They belong to God's Kingdom."

On his way to Jerusalem Jesus stopped in Jericho. The chief tax collector there was Zacchaeus.
He was very short and couldn't see Jesus because of the crowds. So Zacchaeus climbed a tree.
Jesus looked up and said, "Zacchaeus, come down. I'm going to your house today."
From that day on, Zacchaeus was changed. "I will give half my money to the poor," he said.
Jesus was close to Jerusalem now. Outside the city, some friends brought him a donkey.

Jesus sat on the donkey and rode towards Jerusalem. Great crowds of people stood by the road. Some waved branches cut down from the palm trees.

"Hosanna!" the people shouted. "Hosanna! It's the man who comes from God."

The donkey carried Jesus through the streets of Jerusalem to the temple. There Jesus saw many people busy buying and selling. He drove them all out, shouting, "My house should be a house of prayer."

This made the chief priests very angry. They decided to have Jesus killed.

On Thursday of that week, Jesus went to have supper with his friends.

Jesus broke the bread and said, "Take and eat this. It is my body." And he lifted up the cup of wine and said, "Take and drink this. It is my blood."

After supper Jesus and his friends went to the garden of Gethsemane. "Sit here and keep watch while I pray," said Jesus. But his friends fell asleep, leaving Jesus alone.

"Father," Jesus prayed, "save me from this death. But only if that is what you want." Three times he prayed and went back to his friends. But they were still fast asleep.

Suddenly a crowd of people came into the garden, led by Judas, one of Jesus' friends. The people seized Jesus and dragged him to the house of Caiaphas, the chief priest.

"Are you the Son of God?" Caiaphas asked.

"I am," Jesus replied.

"He deserves to die," the people all shouted to Caiaphas.

The priests took Jesus to Pilate, the Roman Governor, and accused him of many things.

"What shall I do with him?" Pilate asked the people.

"Crucify him!" everyone shouted.

"Take him and crucify him then," said Pilate. "I wash my hands of him."

So the soldiers gave Jesus a huge wooden cross.

They made Jesus carry the cross to a hill outside the city.

There they crucified Jesus between two thieves.

His friends placed Jesus' body in a tomb and put a huge stone in front of the opening.

Early on Sunday some women came to the tomb. The stone had been rolled away and the body of Jesus was gone. Two angels were there.

"He is not here," said the angels. "He is alive again."

The women saw a man standing in a garden near the tomb. They thought he was the gardener, but when the man turned around they knew he was Jesus.

"Don't be afraid," said Jesus. "Run and tell my disciples to go up to Galilee. They will see me there."

Jesus' friends were so happy to see him again. He stayed with them for forty days, teaching them about the Kingdom of God.

But Jesus knew that it was time for him to leave this earth. As the sun rose one morning, he went up to his father in heaven.

At the festival of Pentecost, the disciples were all together. Suddenly there was a sound like a rushing wind, and God's power touched them like flames of fire.

Then the disciples went out into all the world to tell people about Jesus and the Kingdom of God.

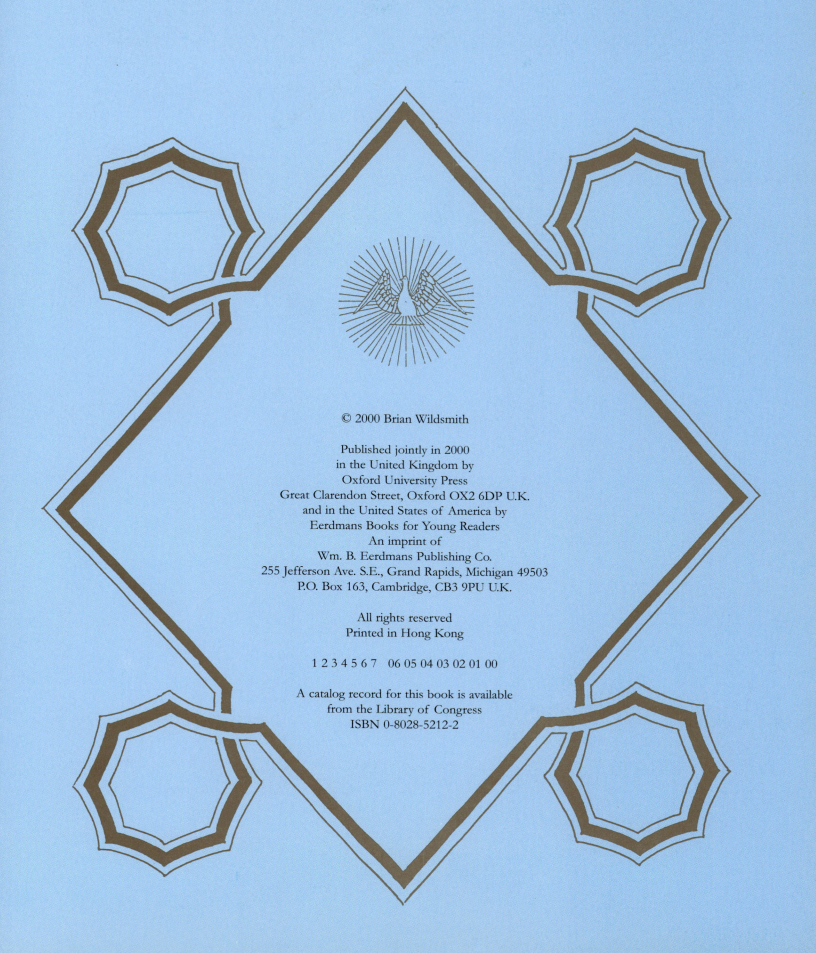

© 2000 Brian Wildsmith

Published jointly in 2000
in the United Kingdom by
Oxford University Press
Great Clarendon Street, Oxford OX2 6DP U.K.
and in the United States of America by
Eerdmans Books for Young Readers
An imprint of
Wm. B. Eerdmans Publishing Co.
255 Jefferson Ave. S.E., Grand Rapids, Michigan 49503
P.O. Box 163, Cambridge, CB3 9PU U.K.

All rights reserved
Printed in Hong Kong

1 2 3 4 5 6 7   06 05 04 03 02 01 00

A catalog record for this book is available
from the Library of Congress
ISBN 0-8028-5212-2